D0375057

⊞ YOU LISTEN NOT TO ANY NOISE WHATSOEVER ALTHOUGH THE MUSIC OF THE STREAM IS THERE. BUT YOU LISTEN TO FALLINGWATER THE WAY YOU LISTEN TO THE QUIET OF THE COUNTRY. ⊞

— FRANK LLOYD WRIGHT
LECTURE AT TALIESIN, 1955

FRANK LLOYD WRIGHT'S
FALLINGWATER

⸬　　C A R L A　　L I N D　　⸬

AN ARCHETYPE PRESS BOOK
POMEGRANATE ARTBOOKS, SAN FRANCISCO

Library of Congress Cataloging-in-Publication Data

Lind, Carla.

Frank Lloyd Wright's Fallingwater / Carla Lind.

p.   cm.   — (Wright at a glance)

"An Archetype Press book."

Includes bibliographical references.

ISBN 0-7649-0015-3 (hc)

1. Wright, Frank Lloyd, 1867–1959 — Criticism and interpretation. 2. Fallingwater (Pa.). 3. Kaufmann family — Homes and haunts — Pennsylvania. I. Title. II. Series: Lind, Carla. Wright at a glance.

NA737.W7A66 1996   96-18138

728'.372'092—dc20   CIP

Published by
Pomegranate Artbooks
Box 808022, Petaluma, CA
94975-8022
Catalogue no. A860

Produced by Archetype Press, Inc.
Project Director: Diane Maddex
Editorial Assistants:
Gretchen Smith Mui and Kristi Flis
Designer: Robert L. Wiser

4 5 6 7 8 9 10
Printed in Singapore

Opening photographs:
Page 1: Frank Lloyd Wright in 1937, the year Fallingwater was completed. Page 2: The house at night, when darkness dissolves the glass. Pages 6–7: The great cantilevers, seen from the side, layered into the lush foliage of the Bear Run valley.

CONTENTS

T HE GREATE/T PER/ONAL AND PROFE//IONAL triumph of Frank Lloyd Wright's distinguished career was the country home he designed in 1935 for Liliane and Edgar J. Kaufmann in a remote area of western Pennsylvania. Fallingwater was a full flowering of Wright's mature theories of organic architecture, sharpened by new-found vitality. Although it stands as a monument to Wright's architectural genius, the house equally marks his dramatic rebirth from a period of chaos and frustration. Through the lens of this one building we can examine the significance of the architect, his work, and his times.

During the preceding two decades Wright (1867–1959) had struggled to bring focus and stability to his career. Constantly on the move, traveling back and forth to Japan, California, Wisconsin, and New York, his personal and financial lives were in turmoil. His Wisconsin home, Taliesin (1911–59), had burned twice and then was confiscated in bankruptcy and divorce litigation. Only five of his commissions were built from 1925 to 1934; his practice struggled for survival. Wright needed publicity and cash to regain his footing.

Wright chose Cherokee red to emphasize—rather than disguise—the metal window frames throughout the house. Creating their own rhythm, they carry a continuous line in contrast to the jagged stone. Fall hues emphasize Wright's favorite color even more.

A REKINDLED CAREER

By 1937 the Taliesin Fellowship had welcomed scores of young architects, among them Byron Mosher and Edgar Tafel (opposite, far right), who supervised Fallingwater. Its completion catapulted Wright to fame and onto the cover of *Time* the next January (above).

WRIGHT CLEVERLY TURNED TO HIS abilities as a communicator, preacher, and teacher. By 1928, at age sixty-one, he had begun a miraculous rejuvenation; his new wife, Olgivanna, thirty years younger, was at his side. With renewed energy Wright began the process of selling himself to the world. In 1932 he published his autobiography, which served to sort out and explain the events of the previous years and to relate his architectural theories. An inspiring and challenging speaker, he welcomed lecture opportunities and encouraged exhibitions of his work.

Also in 1932, in the throws of the Great Depression, the Wrights established the Taliesin Fellowship—survival depended on creativity. Their apprenticeship-based program called for "learning by doing," which in this case meant building and remodeling Taliesin and later Taliesin West (1937–59) in Arizona. The apprentices shared housekeeping, farming, and construction tasks and assisted with whatever architectural work came their way. Wright taught and the students paid, worked, and learned—a mutually rewarding concept.

Edgar Kaufmann Jr. (opposite, left) briefly joined the Taliesin Fellowship in 1934, a relationship that evolved into his role as intermediary between his family and Wright while Fallingwater was being built. He and his father, at right, traveled to Wright's Arizona home, Taliesin West, in the 1950s to visit the architect.

:: Fallingwater was one of those works by Wright that transformed the world's opinion of his art. From seeing a figure of earlier decades he leapt into view as a bold innovator. ::
Edgar Kaufmann Jr.
Fallingwater, 1986

Wright had become more interested in the needs of society at large, was concerned about the increased urbanization of the country, and began speaking about his concept of a decentralized, utopian community he called Broadacre City. The Taliesin apprentices made a model of his futuristic scheme that was first exhibited in New York in 1935.

Edgar Kaufmann was a principal sponsor of this exhibition, the first of many mostly unbuilt Wright projects he would eventually support. Over the years the two talked about a planetarium, planned community, self-service parking garage, house for his son, Edgar Jr., in Palm Springs, California, and for Fallingwater itself a chapel, gate lodge, pool, and television tower.

Kaufmann became the spark that reignited Wright's fire, starting a blazing second career that would last another twenty-five years and yield more than two hundred new buildings. Wright's ability to soar after tragedy exemplifies his resiliency and the durability of his concepts. His rebirth is unparalleled in American architectural history.

CONFRONTING MODERNISM

THE INTERNATIONAL STYLE

WRIGHT WAS CHALLENGED BY THE architectural theories of the 1930s, but he rejected both traditional styles and a new alternative—modernism—offered by the Europeans. Yet the debate may have sharpened Wright's skills and forced him to clarify his designs.

The International Style took hold after a 1932 exhibition at the Museum of Modern Art. Wright disliked its sterility, boxiness, and disregard for the individual and site, although he had contributed to it in part by providing a rationale and model for breaking with tradition.

The architects Walter Gropius and Ludwig Mies van der Rohe of the Bauhaus and Le Corbusier had created a new aesthetic that could not be ignored. It celebrated the machine age, using architectural systems and crisp geometric forms. Austere buildings of glass and steel were seen as an expression of the new industrial society.

Wright disassociated himself from the International Style and recoiled at suggestions that he was influenced by it. He believed in improved technologies and the machine's potential, but he saw them as a means to create desirable buildings, not as an end to which he must conform.

⚏ Fallingwater, Wright's polemic response to modernism, arises from ideas and imagery that flowed in such profusion from his pen and pencil in the years around 1900. ⚏

Joseph Connors
Wright on Nature and the Machine, 1988

Many in Europe considered Wright's work too poetic or spiritual, not rational enough. But as much as he would deny it—cantilevered spaces were in his repertoire three decades earlier—Fallingwater appeared as modern as any of the Bauhaus compositions.

1925 A second fire ravages
Taliesin, Wright's Wisconsin home

1925 The Bauhaus moves from
Weimar, Germany, to a new
school in Dessau (closed by the
Nazis in 1932)

1926–27 Legal problems plague
Wright in his divorce from his
second wife, Miriam Noel; his
personal property is auctioned.
He begins his autobiography

1927–39 Numerous international
awards, lectures, and exhibits high-
light Wright's work

1928 Wright marries Olgivanna
Hinzenberg

1928 Wright writes his "In the
Cause of Architecture" series
for *Architectural Record*

1928 Le Corbusier publishes
Vers une Architecture

1929 Wright builds his temporary
Ocatilla camp in Arizona

1929 The stock market crash
ushers in the Great Depression

1930 Wright challenges European
architectural influences

1932 *An Autobiography* is published
(revised in 1943); the Taliesin Fellowship is formed

1932 The *International Style Architecture Since 1922* exhibition is held
at the Museum of Modern Art

1933–34 The *Century of Progress*
exposition in Chicago emphasizes
modern architecture

1934 Wright visits the Kaufmanns'
waterfall site

1935 Wright's Broadacre City
model is exhibited in New York

1936 Construction of Fallingwater
begins in Mill Run, Pennsylvania

1937 Bauhaus founder Walter
Gropius moves to America

1937 Fallingwater is completed;
Taliesin West and the Johnson
Wax commissions are begun; the
first Usonian house is built

1938 Wright appears on the cover
of *Time* magazine; *Architectural
Forum* is devoted to him; the
Museum of Modern Art opens its
exhibit *A New House on Bear Run*

1939 World War II begins in
Europe

The guest house, built in 1939 on a rise behind the main house,
continues Wright's bold themes. A zigzagging stairway in concrete paints an almost abstract picture against the rough stone.

CAPTIVATED CLIENTS

A RETREAT IN NATURE FOR THE KAUFMANNS

EDGAR J. KAUFMANN (1885–1955) and his wife, Liliane (c. 1885–1952), were wealthy Pittsburgh department store owners, both children of the founders. Edgar, known for his artistic and adventurous spirit and magnetic personality, took over the family business in 1913. Liliane operated a fashionable shop within the store and was a dedicated hospital worker.

The Kaufmanns became interested in Wright's work when they visited their son at Taliesin in 1934. Captivated by Wright's autobiography, Edgar Jr. (1910–89) had applied to be a Taliesin apprentice in search of the spirit it offered. He did not stay long, but the experience changed his life: he eventually joined the design department of the Museum of Modern Art and became a noted design and architecture teacher and author.

Within a month of the Kaufmanns' visit, Wright toured the Mill Run, Pennsylvania, site where they hoped to build a country house in which city people could "renew themselves in nature." Loyal patrons, they kept Wright busy with many projects, but the only others built were an office interior (1935) and Fallingwater's guest house (1939).

⚏ It was an extraordinary moment when the full force of Wright's concept became apparent. . . . Father enjoyed bold ideas and challenges. . . . My mother found sources of graceful livability in an unusual setting. ⚏

Edgar Kaufmann Jr.
Fallingwater, 1986

In the bathroom off the main bedroom, the wash basin is set into an alcove that surrounds it like a window box. Innovative windows throughout the house help blur the distinction between inside and the woodsy outdoors.

THE SITE

ROOTED IN THE EARTH LIKE A TREE

IF FALLINGWATER IS VIEWED AS a perfect marriage of building and site, the leading partner is nature. Wright's habitat is an extension of the Appalachian terrain in which it rests so respectfully. Deep in the rugged forest, where dogwood, rhododendron, oak, maple, birch, and hickory flourish, Bear Run hurries to meet the Youghiogheny River in the valley below.

The Kaufmanns, committed to conservation of the site, regarded the largest of Bear Run's rocky waterfalls as the heart of their property, a place to picnic and lie in the sun. It is here that Wright chose to place the house.

The challenging location in the side of a steep hill gave Wright the southern exposure he preferred and the creative tools he needed. Four giant sandstone boulders became anchors for the house, which was built boldly over the waterfall—not beside it, but above the twenty-foot drop. Layered sandstone ledges were models for the stonework, their projections forecasting the cantilevered decks. The retreat was rooted in the earth, dipped into the stream, looked into the treetops, stretched out like branches from a tree, and used nature's own color palette.

> ⠿ To Wright architecture was a great inclusive agency through which humankind adapted the environment to human needs and reciprocally attuned humankind to its cosmos; amid continual changes, architecture could keep human life more natural and nature more humane. ⠿
>
> Edgar Kaufmann Jr.
> *Fallingwater*, 1986

A rushing Bear Run plays a restful melody off the living area and main bedroom terraces. For two decades before Fallingwater was built, Kaufmann employees enjoyed a camp here, at a former Masonic retreat.

THE CONSTRUCTION

ACHIEVING A DARING VISION

WRIGHT VISITED THE SITE SEVERAL times after Fallingwater's construction began in mid-1936, but he left his young apprentice Byron Mosher, a charter member of the Taliesin Fellowship, in charge of the project. Mendel Glickman provided most of the engineering work, and several other apprentices, particularly Edgar Tafel, contributed along the way. Also an original apprentice, Tafel replaced Mosher for a few months. Mosher returned to see the building completed in late 1937, but Tafel oversaw the fabrication of the extensive custom cabinetry by Gillen Woodworking of Milwaukee.

The long construction was full of challenges, a change of contractor, and debates between Edgar Kaufmann's independent engineers and Wright. One report advised that the site was not suitable for building; others questioned the bearing capacity of the cantilevers and cautioned about cracks in the concrete. Despite his own advisers' concerns, Kaufmann continued to believe in Wright and his unprecedented methods. Kaufmann was an active participant and offered several suggestions, such as the plunge pool that Wright incorporated.

▓ I had no idea I was about to have the privilege of spending one of the most exciting years of my young life gaining experience that would hold me in good stead for decades to follow. ▓

Byron Mosher
In About Wright, 1992

While the poured concrete was curing, Fallingwater-to-be was encased in crude scaffolding. Laborers were recruited from the area and had to be carefully supervised to carry out Wright's experimental methods. Stone for the walls came from the property itself.

Union of building and site

Dramatic siting into a hill, on the boulders of a waterfall, in a forested glen

Expression of the nature of the building materials

Elements used to reveal their essence and character—for example, stone laid as it was naturally stratified and reliance on reinforced concrete for large spans and simple horizontal lines

Central stone core with multiple cantilevers

Outer walls freed to be non-supporting and open to nature through a lavish use of glass

Absence of surface ornament

Clean lines without the austerity and impersonal coldness of the International Style

Flat roofs

Integral to the sweeping horizontality of the design

Geometric composition

Primarily rectilinear forms contrasted with semicircular shapes as a secondary theme

Natural color palette

Warm beiges, golds, and grays, with accents of red

Steel windows

Painted Cherokee red as a defining element in contrast to the earth tones and irregularity of stone

Indirect lighting

Concealed in the ceiling to create soft reflected light

Glass innovations

Invisible corner joints for seamless windows, panes set directly into stone walls, and glass panels reaching to the floor

Spacious, open rooms

A continuous flow of space to outside terraces so that nature becomes a part of the experience of each room

Dramatic contrasts

Intimate alcoves and passageways complementing large open areas

Fine craftsmanship

Custom ironwork and built-in walnut furniture repeating the grammar of the building

Top: Stone walls meet glass straight on or make way for a picturesque boulder. Bottom: Compact shelves mimic the layers of stone, which emphasize horizontality throughout the house.

THE EXTERIOR

▓ Wright believed the cantilever to be the most romantic of all possibilities in structure, and he made the cantilever his main instrument for asserting a new freedom in architecture. ▓

Donald Hoffmann

Frank Lloyd Wright:

Architecture and Nature, 1986

An aerial view clearly shows how far the cantilevered terraces reach out from the central core. At the bottom, hovering over the waterfall, are the living area and the main bedroom. Snaking behind, up the hill, is the walkway to the guest house.

FALLINGWATER'S STRUCTURAL CONCEPT is based on multiple steel-reinforced concrete, cantilevered terraces that extend from a central thirty-foot-tall, layered sandstone core. The first-floor slab dramatically reaches eighteen feet over the water. Wright saw this design as branches of a tree trunk on a hillside.

Pushing technology to create poetry, he used three kinds of cantilever. Wright extended them from an anchor, counterbalanced, and loaded extensions to create a stack of projecting trays, some built around trees. Concrete decks served as floors, and ceilings inside and out were pierced to create trellises and stairways, paved with stone, and inset with lighting. They freed outer walls for generous amounts of glass and liberated interior spaces from interfering supports.

Sandstone for walls and piers was quarried on the site and cut along the natural strata in thin slabs of random lengths. Narrow, recessed mortar joints were nearly invisible. These powerful natural forms provided the vertical strength, visually and structurally, to sustain the horizontal rhythms of the concrete cantilevers.

· 27

⊞ In this design for living down in a glen in a deep forest, shelter took on definite masonry form. . . . ⊞

Frank Lloyd Wright
Architectural Forum, 1938

Wright suggested that the exterior (right) be finished in gold leaf that would mellow to an earthy patina, but Kaufmann objected. Instead, it was coated with a light ochre finish.

Visitors walking to the guest house were protected by an ingenious canopy (pages 30–31), whose curving concrete roof echoes the rising steps of the guests themselves.

Down the driveway, across a bridge, under a trellis—then, finally, visitors encounter the main entrance to Fallingwater (right). Recessed, almost hidden, Wright's cavelike solution entices everyone to find it and enter.

Spaces at Fallingwater flow fluidly from outside to inside, from nature to shelter. The living area bridges the two (opposite), connecting Bear Run and the sky, framed in a clear skylight, with a dramatic staircase plunging right to the water below.

THE INTERIOR

FIRST VIEWED FROM ACROSS THE STREAM, Fallingwater is approached by a narrow bridge. A turn to the left reveals the hidden entry, skillfully detailed to embrace and integrate water into the experience. The living area eventually opens beyond, forty-eight feet long and nearly 1,900 square feet extending to terraces about half as large. Despite the size, it is inviting and comfortable because activity areas are defined within the space. The focal point is the massive stone fireplace, whose hearth is the boulder on which the entire house is centered.

Red steel windows offer a linear counterpoint to the natural-toned, irregular stone walls and the vegetation they frame. Polished flagstone floors continue seamlessly beyond glass walls to large outside terraces. In one corner a hatch opens to a staircase that descends nearly into the run. Another terrace stair leads to a plunge pool, its still waters adjoining the rushing falls.

The kitchen and staff room are tucked behind, into the hill. Upstairs, the main suite and guest room have their own terraces. Another sleeping area and study are on the third level, up in the treetops.

In the third-floor study, only a thin glass membrane separates inside and outside (above). Floor-to-ceiling windows open in and out (opposite), disssolving the corners. A marble sculpture by Hans Arp rests on the desk.

Built-in seating and polished
stone floors tie together the
living areas (pages 36–37).
Their focus is the asymmetrical main fireplace (above and
right). Rising above the floor,
its boulder is a reminder of
Fallingwater's rustic setting.
The red iron kettle swings out
from its nest to heat wine.

Near the living room fireplace—to capture its cozy
warmth—is the house's
modest dining area (pages
40–41). Wright designed a
simple table of walnut veneer,
but the Kaufmanns selected
the imported three-legged
chairs for better stability on
the slick flagstone floors.

The kitchen (left) shares the
serene views of all the rooms
at Fallingwater. Red window
frames direct the eye toward
the head of a Bodhisattva
placed on the terrace off the
living area. More boulders
creep inside, providing a fine
ledge for accouterments.

FURNISHINGS

A PALETTE PROVIDED BY NATURE

Throughout the house, custom furniture of black walnut veneer reiterates the linear cantilevered forms (opposite). Countering these straight lines are curved furniture edges, parapet walls, stair treads, decorative metals, and some wall sections.

Built-in furnishings help streamline the spaces and unify Wright's design themes (pages 46–47). Natural-toned upholstery fabric in the living area offers a simple palette to be spiced up with decorative cushions, pillows, and throws. Nature itself provides the background mural.

THE VARIETY OF DESIGN EXPERIENCES inside Fallingwater is similar to that in the surrounding forest: mysterious paths, sunny glens, winding climbs, precipitous ledges, high overlooks, sheltered coves, filtered light, and earth tones with touches of bright color. Spaciousness flows inside and then out the glass walls, just as the water of the run flows beneath—twisting, cascading, narrowing, broadening, and ever moving.

Within the main room, distinct areas for dining, listening to music, reading, and writing are suggested by the ceiling levels, light decks, furnishings, and walls. Wright designed all of the built-in seating, some stools, the tables, and the cabinetry, but the Kaufmanns controlled most of the other freestanding elements. They rejected some of Wright's designs for lamps, carpets, and chairs. Instead, they selected chairs by contemporary designers and ordered three-legged chairs from Italy for the dining table. Their personal collection of handwoven textiles, carpets, and museum-quality sculpture enhanced the virtuosity of each space's composition. The natural world, the changing seasons, and light contribute the principal ornamentation.

In Kaufmann's third-floor study (opposite) and the stairway leading up to it (left), books on built-in shelves create their own form of integral ornament. The book-lined stair was a special design request from the Kaufmanns to their architect.

⠿ Furnishings should be consistent in design and construction, and used with style as an extension in the sense of the building which they "furnish." . . . The sure reward for maintaining these simple features of architectural integrity is great serenity. ⠿

Frank Lloyd Wright
A Testament, 1957

Another asymmetrical fireplace, this one in the main bedroom, practically becomes the room's far wall. Sturdy ledges provide niches for books and artwork, while the corner desk tucks into the remaining space by the window. To Wright, a fireplace was the heart of every home.

⊞ I have always believed in being careful about my clothes; getting well-dressed because I could then forget all about them. That is what should happen to you with a good house that is a *home*. ⊞

Frank Lloyd Wright

The Natural House, 1954

FALLINGWATER TODAY

ONE OF AMERICA'S MOST FAMOUS HOUSES

IN 1963 EDGAR KAUFMANN JR. generously donated Fallingwater, its 1,543 acres, and an endowment to the Western Pennsylvania Conservancy as the Kaufmann Conservation on Bear Run, a memorial to his parents. He decided against a government, museum, or educational organization in favor of one that would care as much about the site as the building.

Maintenance of the complex building is not without problems. Settlement has required that supports be added, windows replaced and repaired, slabs reworked, and concrete surfaces repaired. Yet Fallingwater stands as proud and visionary as it was six decades ago.

Over the years the house has been visited by many prominent people, including some of Wright's architectural competitors: Walter Gropius, Marcel Breuer, and the Moholy-Nagys. In 1979 a large visitor orientation center was built to facilitate interpretation of the site and now offers guided tours year-round. In one recent year more than 136,000 visitors from all parts of the globe found their way to America's most honored house despite its isolated location on the waterfall over Bear Run.

⊞ This structure might serve to indicate that the sense of shelter . . . has no limitations as to form except the materials used and the methods by which they are employed for what purpose. ⊞

Frank Lloyd Wright
Architectural Forum, 1938

Guests could enjoy their own plunge pool outside the guest house (opposite). Aglow at night (pages 54–55), Fallingwater has been the recipient of numerous awards, most notably inclusion on the American Institute of Architects' list of the most important buildings in America.

Etlin, Richard A. *Frank Lloyd Wright and Le Corbusier.* Manchester: Manchester University Press, 1994.

Hoffmann, Donald. *Frank Lloyd Wright: Architecture and Nature.* New York: Dover Publications, 1986.

————. *Frank Lloyd Wright's Fallingwater: The House and Its History.* New York: Dover Publications, 1978.

Johnson, Donald Leslie. *Frank Lloyd Wright Versus America: The 1930s.* Cambridge: MIT Press, 1990.

Kaufmann, Edgar, Jr. *Fallingwater.* New York: Abbeville Press, 1986.

Pfeiffer, Bruce Brooks, ed. *Frank Lloyd Wright: Monographs. 1924–1936.* Vol. 5. Tokyo: ADA Edita, 1986.

Tafel, Edgar. *About Wright.* New York: Wiley, 1993.

————. *Apprentice to Genius: Years with Frank Lloyd Wright.* New York: McGraw-Hill, 1979.

Wright, Frank Lloyd. *Frank Lloyd Wright: Collected Writings.* Vols. 1–2. Edited by Bruce Brooks Pfeiffer. New York: Rizzoli, 1992.

————. *Letters to Clients.* Selected by Bruce Brooks Pfeiffer. Fresno: California State University Press, 1982.

The author wishes to thank Lynda Waggoner, curator of Fallingwater, and the Carnegie Library of Pittsburgh.

Illustration Sources:
Avery Architectural and
    Fine Arts Library,
    Division of Drawings and
    Archives, Columbia
    University: 22
Chicago Historical Society,
    Hedrich-Blessing Collection:
    1, 10

© Pedro E. Guerrero: 13
© Scott Frances/Esto: 6–7, 17,
    28–29
© Balthazar Korab: 14
© Christopher Little: 2, 8, 19,
    20, 25 top left, 25 bottom
    left, 26, 30–31, 32, 34, 35,
    36–37, 38, 38–39, 40–41,
    42–43, 45, 46–47, 48, 49,
    50–51, 53, 54–55
© Roberto Schezen/Esto:
    25 top right, 25 bottom
    right, 33
© 1938 Time Inc. Reprinted by
    permission: 11

Fallingwater is a house museum open for public visitation. It is located in southwestern Pennsylvania about a one-and-one-half-hour drive from Pittsburgh via the Pennsylvania Turnpike (Donegal exit) and Pennsylvania Route 381, near Ohiopyle. It is open year-round on weekends and also Tuesday through Friday from April 1 to November 15. For further information and reservations, call (412) 329-8501.

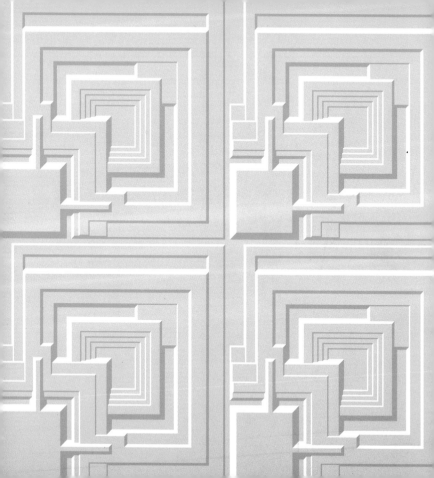